On the Move

MICHAEL ROSEN

On the Move

Home Is Where You Find It

with drawings by
Quentin Blake

CANDLEWICK PRESS

Contents

The War

The Migrants in Me

ON THE MOVE AGAIN

Migrant Poetry

Poetry is the migrant: it travels.
Poetry is the witness: it listens.
Poetry is the survivor: it lasts.

———————

Migration is the story of the human race. Everything we know about history, from the fossil record through to today, shows us that human beings keep moving from place to place.

Sometimes it's for work and sometimes it's for education, but often it's because people have had to escape from where they were living before. They might have woken up to find that their country has changed overnight, perhaps invaded by another country's army, forcing them to run for their lives.

Without warning, they must travel however they can: by foot or by car, by train or by boat, to try to find safety. You may have seen images on TV of people making journeys like this—especially the millions of men, women, and children forced to leave Syria in recent years.

These people are refugees. You might have heard the words "refugees" and "migrants" being used as if they mean the same thing, but it's important to know the difference.

Migrants are people who travel to find a better life—and who could return home without a direct threat to their lives, though it might be to poor conditions. Refugees are people who have been forced to leave their homes and would be in great danger if they tried to go back.

Some people speak about refugees and migrants as if they're bad or dangerous. They seem to think that "normal people" would never find themselves in the wrong place at the wrong time, needing to find a safe place to be.

But migration isn't just something that happens to other people. Chances are, if you look into your own family history, no matter where you come from, you will arrive at the story of your relatives' migration to where you live now.

From the time I was a boy, I knew that people were missing from my family history—aunts and uncles who had been there before the Second World War but weren't there after. And knowing they were gone was linked to a feeling that it would be impossible to find out what had happened to them.

I did know that my aunts and uncles were Jewish, like my family living in London. And, as a teenager, I found out that the party in power in Germany during the war—the Nazis—had organized the murder of six million Jewish people, in what is now known as the Holocaust.

But not only did the Nazis want to "remove" people; they wanted to remove all memory of them, any trace that they ever existed. They wanted my relatives to be wiped from European history.

When I found that out, I was determined to find out what had happened. I was determined to remember them.

I've been writing poems about my family history, and migration, for a long time. Poetry is a way of thinking; it gives me a space to talk about things that are personal to me, but it also lets me leave things hanging in the air . . . and ask questions without giving too-neat answers.

On the Move gathers these poems together for the first time, divided into four sections.

In the first section, there are poems about growing up as part of a Polish Jewish family in London. The second explores how I came to know about the Second World War—which leads into the third section, telling the story of my "missing" relatives. After these very personal poems, I wanted the last section to build a sense of connectedness between my family's experiences and migration around the world.

You also have Quentin Blake's extraordinary pictures to look at. They're "moving" in a different sort of way. I feel moved by the atmosphere they conjure up: the sense of people in danger sticking together, moving on and on.

These pictures could be of people throughout history—on the move during the Second World War, or on the move today . . . because our governments still turn away people with nowhere else to go; because people still "disappear" on dangerous, difficult journeys.

I hope this book shows how we can reach out to one another and share what it is that makes us human. I believe that we are, all of us, citizens of the world, and it seems to me that "home" shouldn't be decided by country borders.

Home is where you find it.

Michael Rosen

Family and Friends

Where Do We Come From?

I come from when houses were ruined,
the skies had stopped exploding,
my father in Germany meeting
the skeleton of a dinosaur in the snow
in the wrecked Berlin Natural History Museum,
my mother holding on to my brother,
having just lost a living, walking, just-talking toddler
to a never-ending cough,
my parents who grew up when you could buy
a live chicken in Hessel Street,
my father sharing his bedroom with his uncle Sam
but never talking to him because one day
Sam had grabbed the cap my father had bought
down Petticoat Lane and turned it inside out.
"Who switched the light off, Father?"
"Neither of us. We didn't have lights.
We had a candle."
My mother having to bring flowers to school
for Harvest Festival but she had no garden,
so she walked down Globe Road
looking for a flower to pick

but there were none,
and there were Mosley's Men out too,
looking for Jews like them to give a beating to
for being Jews,
and the uncles who never came back
from camps in Poland, just vanished, gone,
but I was here, made from all this, all this,
it goes on, it hadn't stopped,
there was my father swearing in Yiddish:
"Chaliera zolste nehmen."
"Don't say that, Harold!" my mum says to him.
And now I can say it too.
And now I can say it too.

Two Languages

Mum can speak two languages
and sometimes mixes them up.
She doesn't say, "Don't moan!"
She says, "Don't kvetch!"
She doesn't say, "Don't slurp your soup!"
She says, "Don't chup!"*

She doesn't say, "Don't burp!"
She says, "Don't graps!"
She doesn't say, "Don't fart!"
She says, "Don't fotz!"

When I have wrinkles in my socks
she says it looks like I've put my feet
through a pile of bagels,
so she says:
"Take the bagels out of your socks!"

So I sing it all back to her:

Don't kvetch,
don't chup,
don't graps,
don't fotz.
Take the bagels
out of your socks.

We all sing it:

Don't kvetch,
don't chup,
don't graps,
don't fotz.
Take the bagels
out of your socks.

* You say "chup" so it nearly rhymes with "soup."

The Songs My Father Sings

When I shut my eyes
and go to sleep,
I think of all sorts of things.
I hear songs, and bits of songs—
songs that my father sings.

How does he know all of these songs?
Where has my father been?
Who sang the songs that he now sings
and what do the songs all mean?

"Et hop, Pipo, Pipo," from France,
"Simsalabim bamba saladu saladim," from Germany,
"Avanti o popolo," from Italy,
"Miss Mary Mack, Mack, Mack," from America,
"Linten adie, toorin adie," from Scotland,
"Mamita mia," from Spain,
"Kalinka, kalinka, kalinka moya," from Russia,
"With a hey, and a ho, and a hey nonny no," from England,

and
"Un di fidldike fidlers,
hobn fidldik gefidlt,
hobn fidldik gefidlt hobn zey,"
from his zeyde.*

When I shut my eyes
and go to sleep,
I think of all sorts of things.
I hear songs, and bits of songs—
songs that my father sings.

* zeyde = grandfather

A Word

I know a word that isn't in the dictionary.
It's a word that comes from my dad.
It's a word that came from his zeyde.
It's a word where I don't really know what it means.
It's a word my father says—and he says
he doesn't really know what it means either.
All he knows is when to say it.
What he knows is when his zeyde
used to say it—his zeyde
who came from far away,
from a place he called "der Heim."*
The word is:
shnobbra-gants.

My father says that his zeyde said it
when there was a big pile of food on the table
and everyone crowded round saying how nice
it was and started to eat it.
I can imagine that:
all the meshpukhe*
crowding round a table,

talking and laughing, and my father is
a small boy trying to get to the table too,
pushing past the meshpukhe,
and his zeyde says . . .
"Shnobbra-gants!"

One day, someone says to me that
"shnobbra" means "beak"
and "gants" means "goose."
"Goose-beak."
At that,
I thought of my father,
all the old relatives turned into geese,
at the edge of a forest
next to a lake,
and they're all
flapping their wings
and honking round the table
and my father turns into a small boy
trying to get to the table,
pushing past the geese.

der Heim = *the old country*
meshpukhe = *relatives*

9

My Father Says

"We would stand by the edge
of the grubby old public swimming pool,
drying ourselves—my zeyde and I.

As likely as not,
he would tell me about
how he would go swimming
back in der Heim, somewhere in Poland.

Always I saw him in a setting
of endless pine trees
and velvet grass, sloping down to a still lake.
It was always early morning.
He would emerge from a log cabin,
run to the water, and fracture
its stillness with strong strokes.
He would go on swimming till he was lost to view.
There were
no other people,
no other houses,
no other movements.

It was a picture I clung to,
from which I had banished
pogroms
and poverty
and fearful people
huddled over their prayers
and sewing machines.

And when we went on day trips to Southend,
East London's seaside,
in his sixties
he would set out to swim the length of the pier
and back, a mile or so each way.
My bubbe,* without fail,
went through the identical torments of anxiety.
'The meshuggener!* He's gone out too far again.'
I was free from all such fears.
For he was always the intrepid boy swimmer
in the pure lake who always came back.

And he did.
And, even in death, still does."

bubbe = *grandmother*
meshuggener = *crazy person*

11

Newcomers

My father came to England
from another country.
My father's mother came to England
from another country,
but my father's father
stayed behind.

So my dad had no dad here
and I never saw him at all.

One day in spring
some things arrived:
a few old papers,
a few old photos,
and—oh, yes—
a hulky bulky thick checked jacket
that belonged to the man
I would have called "Grandad,"
The Man Who Stayed Behind.

But I kept that jacket
and I wore it
and I wore it
and I wore it
till it wore right through
at the back.

Ships

A ship in a bottle
sails down the mantelpiece.
A ship in a photo
brings Granma here.
Ships they talk and talk about.
Ships far and near.

How did the ship
get in the bottle?
Ships by night and by day.
Ships they talk and talk about.
Why did Granma come to stay?

Who put the ship in the bottle?

Ships that they once knew.
Ships they talk and talk about.
Why didn't Grandad come too?

When did the ship
go in the bottle?

Ships sailing far and near.
Ships they talk and talk about.
Who else didn't come here?

Who broke the ship in the bottle?
Can anyone tell me why?
Ships they talk and talk about.
And why did the baby die?

My Friend Ken

Ken lives in Artillery Close.
We stand outside his house
after school, pretending to be singers off the TV,
or the French teacher who is actually French.
We practice doing people's voices and accents.

His dad arrives.
He sits on an electric car,
driving it down Artillery Close.
He waves to us,
driving down the path to the door.
He pulls himself up off the car,
grabs a stick, and walks forward
while he leans back.
He stops to take a breath
by the front door,
gets out his key,
and walks in.

"He was in the Royal Artillery,"
Ken says.

We do a few more singers off the TV,
then I head off to catch the bus—

down Artillery Close.

Bubbe and Zeyde

We sometimes see them on Sunday.
They live in a dark room at the end of a dark corridor
and Bubbe kisses us all when we arrive.
She looks like Mum but very silver and bent at the middle,
which we will all look like one day, says Mum's father.
Dad always looks fed up because he doesn't want to come,
but Mum talks to them properly.
Zeyde looks tired
and pretends that the half crown he's going to give me
disappears into the ceiling along with my nose
if I'm not careful—*snap*—and there's his thumb in his fist,
and he beats me at draughts, dominoes, snap, hare-and-
    hounds,
and even dice,
and he's got a bottle with a boat in it
and we go for walks on Hackney Downs,
which he calls Acknee Dans,
and all the old men there say, "Hallo, Frank,"
and while we're walking along he says:
"What's to become of us, Mickie, what's to become of us?"
and I don't know what to answer.

———

And he shows me to Uncle Hymie,
who looked out of his window and said:
"Is that big boy your grandson, Frank?" (even though
    he knows my name)
because that's the way they talk.
And when we get back we eat chopped herrings or
    chopped liver,
which is my favorite,
and Bubbe tells stories that go on for hours
about people she knows who are ill or people who've
had to pay too much money and at the end of the story
it always seems as if she's been cheated.
And once she took a whole afternoon to tell Mum
how to make pickled cucumber and she kept saying:
"Just add a little salt to taste, a little salt to taste,
just taste it and see if there's enough salt,
to make sure if there's enough salt—just taste and see."
And she calls me "Tottala" and rubs my hair and bites
    her lips
as though I'm going to run away
and so she shakes her head and
says, "Oy yoy yoy yoy yoy."

But Zeyde goes to sleep in the old brown armchair
with his hands on the pockets of his flappy blue trousers
and when we go Mum frowns
and Zeyde holds my hands in his puffy old hand,
keeps ducking his head in little jerks,
and says to us all, come again soon,
but I'd be afraid to go all the way on my own
and it's very dark and the lavatory is outside,
which is sometimes cold.
Bubbe doesn't like it when we go,
and she kisses us all over again
and Dad walks up and down like he does at the station
and Mum keeps pushing me and poking me
and they both wave all the time we go away into the
    distance
and I always wave back because I think they like it
but Mum and Dad sit absolutely quiet
and nobody speaks for ages.
Mum says Zeyde shouldn't give me the money.

Don't Tell Your Mother

When my mum goes to evening classes,
my dad says: "Don't tell your mother,
let's have matzo brei.
She always says,
'Don't give the boys that greasy stuff.
It's bad for them.'
So don't tell her, all right?"

So he breaks up the matzos*
and puts them into water to soften them up.
Then he fries them till they're glazed and crisp.
"It tastes best like this fried in hinne schmaltz,*
skimmed off the top of the chicken soup,"
he says,
"but olive oil will do."

Then he beats three eggs
and pours it on over the frying matzos
till it's all cooked.

Oh, it tastes brilliant;
we love it.

Then we wash everything up,
absolutely everything,
and we go to bed.

Next day, Mum says to us:
"What did your father cook last night?"

There's silence.
We say nothing.

"What did your father cook last night?"
she says again.

"Oh, uh, yeah, you know . . . stuff.
Egg on toast, I think."

matzos = *big flat crackers*
hinne schmaltz = *chicken fat*

My Friends' Eyes

My friends' eyes walk round our flat.
They stop at the paintings:
a Dutch master—a man's head with his hair
in blond ringlets.

Do the eyes see this as strange?

A Brueghel painting of peasants dancing
with bagpipers playing music.

Do the eyes see this as strange?

Another Brueghel painting
of hundreds of people acting out proverbs like
"Who does he think he is?
He thinks he can pee on the moon."

Do the eyes see this as strange?

Their eyes stop at the bookshelves
alongside *The Taming of the Shrew.*
The taming of the shrew.
The taming of the shrew.

Do the eyes see this as strange?

My friends' eyes wander round the table
and wait to see what will come out of the
box that says "Matzos."

Do the eyes see us as strange?

My Friend Robert

Robert asked me over for tea—
"My mum will be pleased to see you again," he said,
because his mum was Mrs. Liebenthal,
the school secretary.

We sat down to eat,
Mr. and Mrs. Liebenthal, Robert, and me.
Mrs. Liebenthal gave us flat wooden plates
and she asked me if I liked rye bread.
I said, "I think so,"
and I put it on the wooden plate.
She said did I like lebkuchen?
I said, "Er . . . I don't really know."
She put a chocolate heart on the wooden plate.
She said did I like pfeffernüsse?
and I said, "I don't really know,"
and she put a pfeffernuss on the wooden plate.

The rye bread was OK.
The lebkuchen was the best chocolate cookie
I had ever tasted.

Really.

The pfeffernüsse, though.

The pfeffernüsse!

Oh, wow!

They were heaven.

Sweet icing, cinnamon cake inside.

I had never tasted anything like it.

"How was that, Michael?" Mrs. Liebenthal said.

"It was really nice," I said.

And she seemed so pleased,

so very pleased,

that I said that

and Mr. and Mrs. Liebenthal

looked at each other

and smiled.

My Friend Roger

My friend Roger says
that I can't walk up the road with him
in case his parents see me,
so I say goodbye to him
at the corner of the road.

But sometimes I just
lean
round
the edge
of the wall
on the corner
and watch him walk up the road
on his own.

The New School

At the new school
two boys sat in front of me
and one said to his friend
(while he pointed at me):
"Don't drop any money on the floor,
he'll only pick it up and keep it."
They both laughed.
I thought, why's that funny?
I thought, if one of them dropped some money,
I would say, "Hey, you dropped some money."

One of them was a very happy boy,
with a bright, round face.
The other one was really clever.
Everyone said he was brilliant at History.

The War

The War

In the evening, after we've eaten,
Mum tells about the War.

"Doodlebugs," she says,
"were bombs that came
flying over us—
rockets, they were,
and they made a noise,
but when the noise stopped
you knew that it was about to drop.
They said you had to run for cover.
If you were out, they said,
the best place to go was in the gutter,
lie down in the gutter.
Once, when I had just come out
of White City Station,
I heard one.
The noise stopped.
They said you had ten seconds to hide
so I ran toward the gutter,
counting to ten,

and I lay down in the gutter and waited.
It landed just up the road from me."

"You lay down in the gutter, Mum? Really?"

In the evening, after we've eaten,
Mum tells about the War.

She says that they thought it wouldn't be long
before Hitler would land in Britain,
but then she tells us about what happened in Russia.
She says the Siege of Leningrad was so bad
and that people got so hungry they ate rats.
She says that people crowded round the radio
because they knew that if Hitler won in Russia
nothing would stop him.
"If he had come here," she says,
"we wouldn't be alive.
You wouldn't have been born," she says to me.

They listened to the reports of the
Battle of Stalingrad.

"You see," she says,
"Hitler's troops were lined up here . . ."
And she starts moving the plates
and jugs and sauce bottle round the table.
"The Russians were here.
There was a moment when we thought
it was all over and the Russians had lost
and it would be all over for us.
But then, look"—
she moves the jugs and plates again—
"they won!
We couldn't believe it."

She stops.
She stares.
They lost millions.
Millions and millions of people died.

In the evening, after we've eaten,
Mum tells about the War.

Skeletons

My dad was in Berlin in 1946
and his old friend David
said that a friend of his was
at the Berlin Natural History Museum.
David wondered if he was still there.

At the time
Berlin was under a foot of snow,
the roads were covered with snow,
there was scarcely anything going along them.
You could scarcely see where the roads went.

My dad says he walked for hours
through heaps of bomb rubble and snow,
round huge craters in the ground,
under walls leaning over.

Snow everywhere.
Till suddenly, he came face-to-face with
some enormous skeletons in the snow.

The old Berlin Natural History Museum
had been hit by a bomb.
There were dinosaur skeletons
standing there in the middle of nowhere.
Great bones and skulls
rising up out of the snow
amongst heaps of broken brick
and broken glass.

"I'll never forget the sight
of those dinosaur skeletons,"
my dad says.

I've never forgotten them, either—
though I never saw them.

Bratwurst

We went to Berlin
and it was only twelve years
after the end of the war.

I discovered bratwurst,
a kind of hot dog that
you could buy from a kind of stall
on the street, and you could have it
"mit oder ohne Senf"—
"with or without mustard."
And the mustard was a kind of mustard
you couldn't get in England then:
sweet and spicy.
I always said, *"Mit Senf, bitte.*
With mustard, please."
I loved *Bratwurst mit Senf.*

My brother loved taking photos.
He said that he really wanted to see
Hitler's bunker
and he would take a photo of it.

"What's that?" I said.
"It was where Hitler was staying
at the end of the war," he told me.
"It was like an underground house.
The Russians were getting nearer and nearer
and Hitler and the rest committed suicide in there."

Sure enough, one day,
we were in a bus and the bus went past
a pile of rubble and sticking up out of the ground
was a huge chunk of concrete.
I said I thought it looked like
a massive triangle of cake
tipped up on its side.
Mum frowned.
My father shrugged.
"It's tipped up like that,"
my brother explained,
"because that's where a bomb hit it."
I said,
"When the bus stops,
can I go and get some
Bratwurst mit Senf?"

My Friend Mart

On holiday, in Wales,
when we're camping,
on Butler's Farm by the River Monnow,
Mart's dad, Fred, gets into his shorts
and puts on a khaki shirt,
puts on his boots
and gets busy with the tents.
"Anyone want tea?" he says.

He makes us all tea and pours his
into his old army cup.
Then he sits down,
turns to the rest of us,
and starts talking in Italian.
"That's Italian," he says.
Then he gets up,
takes the cups over to the bowl,
washes them up,
and hangs them up to dry.

I say to Mart,

"Why was your dad talking Italian?"

"He was in Italy during the war," Mart says.

"Eighth Army."

"What did he do?" I say.

"I don't really know," Mart says.

I sit and wonder why it was the *eighth* one.

What about the other armies?

What did they do?

France

I was at a ceremony in France
in the middle of some fields,
next to a wood
at a place by the side of the road.
There was a plaque with a man's name on it.
Lots of people from a village nearby
were there: some men stood with flags,
and they played the French national anthem.
A man spoke and said that it was here
that some people from the Resistance
had tried to escape.

(As he said that, some cows in the field
started to moo really loudly,
so he had to speak up more.)

With the people was a young doctor called
Kopkiowski—and though he managed
to look after the others,
one of the men died.

Later, we went up into the hills
and saw a big old house,
behind some trees . . .
and this was a secret hospital
that two young Jewish doctors from
the big town nearby had set up,
in case Resistance people got injured.

Now it was part of a farm.
No sign.
Just chickens.

And a dog.
There's always a dog.

Utah Beach

Monsieur Piat stands on the beach,
his eyes disappearing into his face.

Jacques and Mart are playing football.
Claudine and Nicole are racing.

He takes me to the back of the beach,
where the dry grass waves in the wind.

Monsieur Piat points to some words
written on a metal plate.

The sign explains that on this beach,
thousands of men jumped out of boats
and ran toward a gun that was placed
right where we are standing.

Hundreds of men died.

Monsieur Piat has a dent in his leg.
His eyes disappear into his face.

Counting

When they do war,
they forget how to count.
They forget how to count,
and that's how they do it.

They come,
they kill;
they kill,
they go.

No numbers.
No names.
They disappear them.
They vanish them.
That's how they do it.

They come,
they kill;
they kill,
they go.

And it's
"worth it,"
they say,
"it's worth it, believe us,"
if you forget how to count.

If you forget the numbers.
If you forget the names.
If you forget the faces.

When they do war,
they forget how to count.
They forget how to count,
and that's how they do it.

But we're counting.
Watch us:
we're counting.
Listen.
We're counting.
And
we count.

The Migrants in Me

The Absentees

There are gaps,
there are blanks,
in the house
of my life;
there's a face,
nothing more,
something gone
from my life.

She was here,
he was there,
in the rooms
of my life;
there's a place
for them both
in the words
of my life.

The French Uncles

Every now and then
my father would say,
"I had two French uncles.
They were in France
at the beginning of the war.
They weren't there at the end."

"What happened to them?" we'd say.
"Don't know," he'd say.
"All I know is that they were there
at the beginning of the war,
and they weren't there at the end."

Finding Out

For years I tried to find out
what happened to my father's uncles.
All I had were scraps, words, names,
floating in front of me like leaves
falling off trees:
Oscar, Martin, Metz, route de Thionville,
dentist, clock mender . . .

One day, my cousin in America wrote:
a distant relative had died.
In his papers
there were two letters
from one of the uncles, Oscar,
and two letters
from his sister in Poland, Stella,
all written during the war
and asking for help.

I pored over the letters,
trying to give the words
a voice that I could hear.

Now that I had addresses,
the internet
and books
and museums
were kinder,
they gave me more and more.
Now I could make maps
where the uncles went,
where they ran to,
where they hid,
where they were seized and taken to.

Then, one day, another email
arrived from my cousin in America.
His father and stepmother had died
and he had just been in the house.

"I noticed there was a closet," he said.
"It was locked, so I opened it. I could see
it was full of photos. There was a sealed-up box
in there. On the box, it said, 'Family Photos.'
I cut it open and inside there were old black-
and-white photos with names on them:

Oscar and Martin.
And many more.
They've been there for years and years.
I'll send them to you right now."
And he did.

Now I could see Oscar and Martin.
I could see their faces
and what Oscar looked like
in his First World War army uniform.
There were more places, like Bielitz,
more names of brothers and sisters,
and photos of their father and mother.
These were my great-grandparents
in New York
over a hundred years ago!

Pictures I had never seen.
Pictures my father had never seen . . .
"But why," I said to my cousin in America,
"was the closet locked?
Why were the photos in a sealed-up box?"

I had sat in that room with the closet
behind me and I had asked his father
about Oscar and Martin,
what did he know?

And all the time the photos were sitting
just a few feet away.
And all he had been able to give me were
falling leaves.

Nothing

Some of you know nothing.
From you there is nothing.

Some of you know something.
From you there is nothing.

Some of you know a lot.
From you there is nothing.

You can't speak of it.
It is the unspeakable.

You can't say it.
It is the unsayable.

You can't say what you know.
It is the unknowable.

Dear Oscar and Rachel

Oscar and Rachel,
you escaped from where
they pinned a yellow star
on you.
You escaped from where
they took all you had.
You escaped from where
they made you put a sign
on your market stall
saying "Jewish business."

Oscar and Rachel,
you heard it was safe
in the great resort of Nice
on the other side of France,
because the Italians in Nice
were refusing to send Jews like you
away on trains to the east,
to a place no one was coming back from.
So you both ran
all the way there.

Oscar and Rachel,
in Nice,
the Italians put you in a grand old hotel.
You were waiting in that hotel,
thinking you were safe.
Thinking you were about to get on board
and sail away, across the sea to North Africa,
and you would be safe till the war was over.

Until you saw the Italians leave.
Until you saw one of the worst,
most violent Nazis of all
march into Nice.
Until his police
found a few thousand of you
waiting in the hotel,
and wrote your names down
and put you on a train to Paris,
and then on a train to the east,
where no one was coming back from.

Oscar and Rachel,
you were so close,
so near
to the waves that would take you away,
so near
to where the war couldn't reach you.

I sometimes think how
on holidays in France
when I was a boy,
I might have met you,
Oscar and Rachel.

And I would have listened to you telling stories
about your great escape
across the sea.

Dear Oscar

What did you think,
as you and Rachel
sat on the floor of the cattle truck
as it left Paris?

Did you think
of the watches and clocks you had mended?
Did you think
of the tiny springs and wheels?
You, with your magnifying glass in your eye,
poring over the works
so that a Monsieur or a Madame
could tell the time,
correct to the exact second?

Did you think
of the smell of the sea
and the push of a boat
against the waves?
How you and Rachel
would stand on the deck,
the wind in your faces,
as you sailed away?

Did you look through
the gaps in the slats
on the side of the truck?
Did you see farmers in fields?
Women selling clothes in a market?
Did you call out?
Did you push your hands through the gaps?

Did the night come creeping in?
Did you see a light from a window
where people sat
and ate their evening meal?

Did you see, in the dark,
horror on Rachel's face?
Did she see horror on yours?
Did you shut her eyes?
Did she shut yours?
Thinking of children
who shut their eyes
to make the world go away?

And then behind your eyelids
did you think of the cattle
that had once stood in the truck
as they were taken away
to the slaughterhouse?

Compassion

I read an article
about the train
that took my great-uncle and my great-aunt
Jeschie* and Rachel to Auschwitz:
Convoy 62.
The article said
that some of the prisoners on Convoy 62
escaped from the train
while it was in a tunnel.

One of the prisoners was called
Oscar Handschuh,
and when he jumped from the train,
he knocked himself out.

After a bit, he came round and headed off
into the countryside.
He arrived at a farm and asked for help.
The people there were called
Mariette and Marcel Médard.
They bandaged his head, gave him clothing
and food, and hid him in an attic.

That day, German soldiers came to the farm.
They said they were looking for ten Jews
who had jumped from a train.

Marcel Médard said that there was no one
in the house.

A long while later, the war ended—
and for many years, the Handschuh family stayed
in touch with the Médard family.

Why?
Because Oscar Handschuh knew,
and the Médard family knew,
that if Oscar Handschuh had been found by the
soldiers that day,
he would have been killed,
and the Médard family would have been killed.

All of them.

* A nickname for Oscar Rosen

Martin Rozen, My Father's Uncle

In the early hours of January 31, 1944,
four French policemen
knocked on the door of Madame Bobières
in the village of Sainte-Hermine in the Vendée.

Later the policeman in charge
wrote a report explaining
what happened next:
"Martin Rozen opened the door."
He was,
the report said,
"born on August 18, 1890
at Krośniewice in Poland.
Jeweler, son of Jonas and Rachel,
naturalized French, Jewish race.
1 meter 62
brown eyes
oval face
straight nose
regular mouth
dressed in yellow cotton trousers

and gray cotton jacket
wearing a Basque beret and low-heeled shoes.
Scar on his left cheek.
He was taken to the parish hall at La Roche-sur-Yon."

What they didn't go on to say
was that this was the first step on a journey
that would take Martin Rozen
first to Drancy, the prison for Jews,
and then to a station called Paris-Bobigny,
where he would be put in a cattle truck
and sent to Auschwitz,
where he was killed.

Though these facts are missing,
the writing is very neat.
In fact,
everything seems to have been done properly.

Whose Fault?

I look at the names of the police
who knocked on the door
of my father's uncle
in the middle of the night
and arrested Martin.

Here they are:
Eugène Cabanetos,
Arnand Mazouin,
Georges Salomon,
and their officer in charge,
Pierre Le Papu.

Is it their fault?

They were ordered to arrest him
by *Gaston Jammet,* the subprefect,
who was following the orders
of *Louis Bourgain,* the prefect.

Louis Bourgain was following
the orders of
Hermann Herold,
the local German commander
of the security police.

He was following the orders
of:
René Bousquet,
secretary-general responsible
for the French police,
and *Carl Oberg*,
Higher SS and police leader,
based in Paris,
who was under the command of
Adolf Eichmann
(who was in charge of organizing
the trains that transported
Jews to the concentration camps),
who was under the command of
Heinrich Himmler,
who was under the command of
Adolf Hitler, the leader of Nazi Germany.
But why were
Hermann Herold
and *Carl Oberg*
in France?

Because Nazi Germany invaded France
and "occupied" it.

Why did they do that?

Because Adolf Hitler figured out
that he couldn't expand Germany into
Eastern Europe
until he had defeated
Western Europe.

But why did they round up millions of Jews
from Germany and the countries they "occupied"
and send them to concentration camps
to be killed?

Because the Nazis believed
that this was the right thing to do.

But how did people with such
monstrous ideas get into power?

Yes, good question.
How did they?

Late at Night

Late at night,
I'm groping through the internet,
and I find that my father's uncle Oscar
fought in the First World War
in the Kaiserlich und Königlich* Infantry Regiment 56.
It's a Polish regiment that fought
alongside the German army
in the Austro-Hungarian army.

Another night,
I find that my father's uncle Martin
fought in the First World War
in the Deuxième Régiment Étranger.*
It's a French regiment that fought
against the Austro-Hungarian army.

After the First World War,
they lived near each other in France—
near enough for Martin
to be best man
at Oscar's wedding.

Fighting with the German army
didn't save Uncle Oscar.
He was deported from France by
the German security police
to Auschwitz
and never came back.

Fighting with the French army
didn't save Uncle Martin.
He was arrested by the French police,
handed over to the German security police,
deported to Auschwitz,
and never came back.

* Kaiserlich und Königlich = King's Own
* Deuxième Régiment Étranger = Second Foreign Regiment

Yours Hopefully

Meine Lieben,*
my dears,
we have hopes,
we have fears.

So send us news.
Send us a word.
Please send for our brothers,
send for our mother.
Nothing more can be said,
as this letter may be read by others.

Dear sisters,
from your brothers,
between us such a distance,
meine Lieben, ambestens.*
I close this letter
hoping, with you,
tomorrow will be better,
meine Lieben, my dears.

> * *meine Lieben = my dears (pronounced "my-na lee-bun")*
>> * *ambestens = best wishes (pronounced "um-bestence")*

Cousin Michael

There was a wedding,
and we were invited
and, when we got there,
there was a man
who they said was
my father's cousin.

This is Michael, they said—
same name as you, *hah*!
And at one point in the
wedding, my aunt took
me to one side and said
that there was a time
during the war when
Michael was a boy,
sixteen or seventeen,
no older than you are now,
she said, and his parents
said to him that it
wasn't going to be
safe where they were

in Poland.
And so, my aunt said,
his parents put him on
a train and he never
saw them again.

Like it always was,
at that time, when
people told me things
like this, my aunt just
shrugged, looked sad,
and said, I suppose
they died in the camps,
and I never knew what
that meant—what were
these camps? Why were
people taken there?

At the wedding,
I watched him.
He must have been about
forty years old then.
In my mind, I thought of him

being the same age
as me, and I imagined
my parents
saying to me one day:
Michael, go, don't stay,
there are soldiers
and police and they are
kicking us out of our
houses and flats—
go, don't stay.
So they come with me
to a station and we
wait for a train and
all the time we are looking
out for soldiers and
police, but it's OK, so they
hug me and kiss me
and I get on the train,
and stand in the
corridor and wave to them
through the window,
and I can see them close
together, waving, and then

there's a shout and a whistle
and the train starts to pull off
and they wave and they wave
and I wave and I wave
till they're gone.

And that's the last I ever see
of them. I never see them again,
but wherever I go, and whoever
I'm with, I remember that picture
of them standing together,
waving me off, and for the rest
of my life I can't make any of it
make sense, that they did that
thing of making me safe and
there was nothing they could
do for themselves. And I think
again and again of what they
might have been thinking at
that moment, as they waved
and stood close to each other.
What did they think as they
lost everything? And later

they were herded together
and taken to a camp, never knowing
what had happened, never knowing
why this was happening, never knowing
what happened to me,
even at the very end
as they were closing their eyes.

And though I smile and walk about
in the world, I carry this with me
wherever I am, whoever I'm with,
and no matter how many times
I try to change it, no matter
how many times I try to get them
to come with me on the train,
or how many times I get them
to escape and find me in those
freezing places where I ended up,
or how many times I imagine
that I meet them after the War
is over, and we hug and kiss
and cry, it never happens.
It never happens. There

is always nothing. Nothing but
nothing.

But I walk about in the world
smiling and nodding. I even go
to weddings, and people smile
at me, even this young man
with the same name as me,
no older than I was then when
my parents put me on the train.

And he's looking at me
like he's trying to
read me
like a
book.

Leosia

I went to see my father's cousin Michael.
He was born in Poland.

When the Nazis came in the west
his parents put him on a train
going east
and he never saw them again.
They died in a Nazi death camp.

When the Russians came in the east
he was arrested, put on a train,
and sent to one of the Russian camps.
But he lived.

When I went to see him
he wouldn't tell me any of this.
When he went out of the room
his wife said he can't bear to talk about it.
When he came back into the room
he said, "Tell him the story about my cousin Leosia."

So they told me the story about Cousin Leosia.

"When the Nazis came in the west
Leosia pretended to be a Christian.
She put a crucifix around her neck
and then she fetched her grandmother's brooch
and took the diamonds off it.
She took the soles off the heels of her shoes,
put the diamonds inside the heels,
and put the soles back on.
She thought if there were going to be any problems
she would be able to sell them.
Then she went west
into Germany.

In Germany she worked in a factory.
No one ever found out that she was Jewish.

At the end of the war
she couldn't face going back to Poland.
Her parents, all her friends, and all her relations
had been taken away to the camps and killed.

She went to Israel to find her brother Naftali.

She told him how she had lived
right through the war
with diamonds in the heels of her shoes.
'I already knew if ever I got into difficulty
I could've sold them
and maybe paid someone to help me.
And here they are,' she said, 'the very diamonds themselves.'

And Naftali said, 'Where did you get the diamonds from,
Leosia?'
And Leosia said, 'From our grandmother's brooch.'
So Naftali said, 'Listen carefully, Leosia.
Many years ago, our grandmother wrote to me.
She said that Grandfather's business wasn't doing too well
and so to help out
she had taken the diamonds off her brooch,
put in glass ones instead,
and sold off the diamonds.
She didn't tell anyone about it
but she wrote to me to get it off her chest.
You went through the whole war

with nothing more than
bits of glass in the heels of your shoes.'"

When the story was finished, someone listening said,
"It just goes to show what you can do with a bit of
confidence!"

Arriving

The guns stopped.
The bombs stopped.
The world was broken.
People were broken.
Millions of people had no home,
millions of people were far from home.

One of them was called Michael.
He was alone.
No father, no mother.
Alone amongst millions.
What now?
He had an address.
He had a cousin in England.

So, one day,
some time after the guns and bombs
had stopped,
a woman called Sylvia was in her house
when the doorbell rang.

Out of all the family
out there,
where the camps had been,
he was the only one
who had survived.
Now he was standing on the
doorstep.
He was the only one
who had arrived.

And he stayed and stayed.
And where he stayed
he made his home.

Today; One Day

Today

The rain has died

My shoes have died

The sun has died

My coat has died

The Earth has died

Today.

One day

The rain will flower

My shoes will laugh

The sun will sing

My coat will fly

The Earth will dance

One day.

On the Move
Again

Never Again

We say, "Never again."

But
when people with power are pointing
in one direction
when many minds are pointing
in that direction
when the guns and bombs are pointing
in that direction
too,
it can happen again.
It does happen again.
It has happened again.
It can be furious and chaotic.
It can be calm and orderly.
It can start with laws.
It can start without them.

The people who do it
can believe
they are saving their country.

The people who do it
can believe
that they are just getting
their own back.

That's why
it can happen again.
It does happen again.
It has happened again.

Don't Drown

Don't drown.
Practice swimming for a long, long time.
Don't drown.
Practice shouting, "Help!"
Don't drown.
Keep the water out.
Don't drown.
Call for help.
Don't drown.
If you see the water rising, leave.
Don't drown.
If you think you're sinking, grab something.
Don't drown.
If you think there's no way out,
you're probably wrong and there is a way out. Find it!
Don't drown.
If you think you're stuck, probably you're not.
Don't drown.
If you think you can't go on, probably you can.
Don't drown.

Water

Water slips through my hands,
falling and falling away.
It twists and turns and slides,
it can't stop or stay.

Pictures in my mind of you,
they slip and fall away.
Twisting and turning and sliding,
till they are gone too.

There's water in the river.
There's water in the sea.
I reach out to touch it.
The water touches me.

Water slips through my hands,
falling and falling away.
It twists and turns and slides,
it can't stop or stay.

Homesickness

Once upon a time I was in a story
where I met an invisible thing
who said that I could have one wish
and I said that my wish was that
I could go back to the place and time
I miss the most
and the invisible thing said that I could.
But:
though I could go back to the *place*
I could never go back to that *time.*
Then I pleaded with the invisible thing
and said, "Please can it be both,
the place and the time?"
And the invisible thing said,
very well it could,
but if I did go back to that place and time,
I must promise not to speak to anyone
in that place.
"What will happen if I do?" I said,
and the invisible thing said that
if I did, I would never get back to now.

I agreed and in a flash
I was there and then
in that place and in that time:

It was winter,
there were my friends,
the ice on the pond was thick enough
to carry them sliding and shouting
all morning
and we felt the ice with our fingers.

Then it was spring,
the birds in an orchard whistled
through the blossoms
and I brushed a branch with my fingers.

Then it was a summer evening, just a gust of wind
raised dust in the alley where my friends kicked a ball.
I was in goal and the ball smacked my hand till it stung.

Then it was autumn
and we lined up in rows in silence,
waiting for orders to walk in single file to class
and I touched the shoulders of the boy in front.

But I didn't speak to anyone.

And then I was at a station,
waiting for my mother to come home
from work.
The trains rolled in and out
and when the woman in the kiosk
asked me if I wanted some sweets
I remembered not to answer her
and another train pulled in, the doors
opened and I could see my mother
step down onto the platform
and when she reached me,
she put her arm round me
and said, "There's no need for you
to wait for me here, you've got a key,
you can let yourself in,
why don't you go home?"

And I shrugged and said, "I like waiting
here ..."
And she held my hand.

And the invisible thing whispered
in my ear,
"You've spoken."
"I know I have," I said.
"You'll be here forever and ever,"
it said.
And I said,
"But you're just an invisible thing in a story.
I can decide what I'll do.
You can't rule over me."
And the invisible thing laughed.
"You're right. You're totally right
and I am wrong.
You will be able to get back."
I laughed too,
and I said,
"And I will be able to come here again."

But the invisible thing spoke again:
"You're right about it all,
but for one thing."
"What's that?" I said.
"Yes, you can travel to and fro
between here and there,
between then and now,
just as you want.
But without me,
when you go to the place and time
that you miss the most
you won't be able to touch anything.

Not a thing."

Gone

She sat in the back of the van
and we waved to her there
we ran toward her
but the van moved off
we ran faster
she reached out for us
the van moved faster
we reached for her hand
she stretched out of the back of the van
we ran
reaching
the van got away
we stopped running
we never reached her
before she was gone.

Overheard in a Classroom

He doesn't speak English, Miss.

He comes from the Congo, Miss.

I translate for you, Miss.

He says that the bad men take his grandfather, Miss.

He says that the bad men take his grandmother, Miss.

He says that the bad men take his dad, Miss.

He says that the bad men take his mum, Miss.

He doesn't say how he got here, Miss.

He can't say how he got here, Miss.

My Dad

My dad is a map:
follow this road
cross this bridge
go round this lake
don't fall down this cliff
climb this hilltop
and look at this view.

Today
I've got to follow this road
cross this bridge
go round this lake
not fall down this cliff
climb this hilltop
and look at this view
without a map.

Where?

He said,
"I can't stand it anymore.
It's doing me head in.
This place used to be like a village.
It's full of foreigners," he said.
"I love Walthamstow," he said,
"but I can't stay here.
I'm going," he said.

So I said, "Where? Where are you going?"
And he said,
"Spain."

English Literature

I studied English Literature.
"We start at the beginning," they said,
"with *Beowulf*, written a thousand years ago
in Old English," they said,
"so you had better learn Old English."

Beowulf was so old
that the Old English it was written in
was like Old Dutch or Old German.
"Look in the back of the book for notes,"
they said.
It turns out that no one in *Beowulf*
was English.

Later, we read Chaucer.
"This is when modern English Literature
begins," they said.
"Read the notes at the back, it'll help you,"
they said.
Turns out that some of the stories
came from Italy, some came from France,

and the whole idea of the book being
people telling stories
came from Arabic books.

Later, we read Shakespeare.
"This is the greatest writer of
English Literature," they said.
"Look at the notes at the back," they said.
Turns out that some of the stories
came from Italy, from ancient Greece
and ancient Rome, and from Scandinavia,
with bits from the Bible throughout.
And the Bible was originally from the Middle East.

Later, we read books
by Emily, Anne, and Charlotte Brontë.
They were born in England.
Their father came from Ireland.
Later, we read Oscar Wilde,
who came from Ireland,
Bernard Shaw,
who came from Ireland,
and Joseph Conrad,
who came from Poland.

Then it stopped.
We weren't allowed to go on
after 1900.
Otherwise I might have
studied
T. S. Eliot (American),
James Joyce (Irish),
Chinua Achebe (Nigerian),
Jean Rhys (Dominican),
or Derek Walcott,
who came from Saint Lucia.

So there you have it:
English Literature.

The Migrants in Me

Maybe I look as if
you could spin a story at me
about how threatening
and dangerous migrants are,
as if neither I nor you would ever dream
of upping sticks and living somewhere else
and being, you know, a migrant.
As if neither I nor you
might suddenly find ourselves
in a wrong place at a wrong time
carrying the wrong passport,
with a face that doesn't fit,
and needing to get out,
move, find a safe place because,
what, is it only mad, bad, and sad people
who do that sort of thing,
and neither I nor you
is mad, bad, or sad enough?

No, don't think you can take
the migrants out of me.

The migrants in me tell me
about crisscrossing Europe,
about crisscrossing the Atlantic.
They warn me—they *remind* me—
of long, long hours at workbenches.

They remind me of relatives
who at one moment
were as safe as houses,
and the next,
had no houses to be safe in.

Everyone Comes from Somewhere

Everyone comes from somewhere.
Everyone has a past.
Everyone is somewhere first.
Everyone is somewhere last.

Deep in the heart of buildings
scattered about online
packed away in boxes
hiding in cupboards
are fragments and hints
about your life and mine.

You catch a glimpse of your name,
you might suddenly see an address;
sometimes it's typed,
because your name was recorded by an official;
sometimes it's writing that looks like
it was written by spiders.

Everyone comes from somewhere.
Everyone has a past.
Everyone is somewhere first.
Everyone is somewhere last.

These are the stones on a path:
a story
of how people travel.
These are the stones on a path
that I found,
the story that I unraveled.

Everyone comes from somewhere.
Everyone has a past.
Everyone is somewhere first.
Everyone is somewhere last.

On the Move Again

You know
you gotta go.
No time to grieve.
You just gotta leave.
Get away from the pain.
On the move again.

Take the train.
Catch a plane.

Make the trip
in a ship.

Take a hike.
Ride a bike.

Go by car.
Going far.

Use your feet
on the street.

Get stuck
in a truck.

Then you arrive
and you're alive.

You arrive.
You're alive.

What you leave behind
won't leave your mind.

But home is where you find it.
Home is where you find it.
Home is where you find it.
Home is where you find it.

Today

You can't do something yesterday.
You can't do something tomorrow.
You can only do something now.
You can remember something from yesterday.
You can plan something for tomorrow.
You can only do something now.

What you did yesterday
can help you choose what to do now.
What you did yesterday and what you do now
can help you plan what to do tomorrow.
But you can only do something now.

Resources and How to Help

Now that you've read this book, I hope you will keep thinking about the topics raised and the unanswered questions in the poems.

There are all kinds of ways in which we can help refugees and people affected by displacement. Below are a few resources that may prove useful.

Charities and organizations supporting refugees:
You can find out more about the refugee crisis, as well as advice on how to get involved, on these websites:

- **UNHCR** (The UN Refugee Agency)—www.unhcr.org
- **HIAS**—www.hias.org
- **RAICES** (The Refugee and Immigrant Center for Education and Legal Services)—www.raicestexas.org
- **The Young Center**—www.theyoungcenter.org
- **Human Rights Watch**—www.hrw.org/topic/refugee-rights
- **International Refugee Assistance Project**—https://refugeerights.org
- **International Rescue Committee**—www.rescue.org

- **World Food Programme**—www.wfp.org
- **Amnesty International**—www.amnesty.org/en /what-we-do/refugees-asylum-seekers-and-migrants
- **ACLU** (American Civil Liberties Union)— www.aclu.org/issues/immigrants-rights
- **Make the Road New York**—https://maketheroadny .org
- **Cosecha**—www.lahuelga.com

You can also look up the **Tenement Museum** (www .tenement.org) and the **Pacific Coast Immigration Museum** (www.pacificcoastimmigrationmuseum.org/index.html) for more about migration to and within the United States.

Charities and organizations for Holocaust education:
I wrote about my family's experience of the Holocaust, and the story of how I found out what happened to them, in *The Missing: The True Story of My Family in World War II* (Candlewick Press). You can find out more about the Holocaust through these organizations:

- **The Anne Frank Center for Mutual Respect**— www.annefrank.com

- **The Holocaust Educational Trust**—www.het.org.uk
- **Mémorial de la Shoah** (The Shoah Memorial)—www.memorialdelashoah.org/en
- **The United States Holocaust Memorial Museum**—www.ushmm.org
- **The Wiener Holocaust Library**—www.wienerlibrary.co.uk
- **Yad Vashem: The World Holocaust Remembrance Center**—www.yadvashem.org

Audio:

I have also recorded poems about my family's experience of the Holocaust and poems about racism and prejudice; these recordings are freely available via Historyworks on Audioboom:

audioboom.com/playlists/4613930-michael-rosen-poems

ACKNOWLEDGMENTS

"Skeletons," "Newcomers," and "Bubbe and Zeyde," were reproduced from *Quick, Let's Get Out of Here!* by Michael Rosen (Puffin). Copyright © by Michael Rosen 1983. "Where Do We Come From?," "Today; One Day," "Don't Drown," "My Dad," and "On the Move Again" were reproduced from *Michael Rosen's Big Book of Bad Things* by Michael Rosen (Puffin). Copyright © by Michael Rosen 2010. "Leosia," "My Friend Roger," and "Don't Tell Your Mother" were reproduced from *You Wait Till I'm Older Than You* by Michael Rosen (Puffin). Copyright © by Michael Rosen 1996. "Two Languages," "Songs My Father Sings," "A Word," and "Ships" were reproduced from *Jelly Boots, Smelly Boots* by Michael Rosen (Bloomsbury, 2016) and are printed by permission of Bloomsbury Publishing Plc on behalf of Michael Rosen. "The Migrants in Me" was first published in *Don't Mention the Children* (Smokestack Books, 2015) and *Listening to a Pogrom on the Radio* (Smokestack Books, 2017) by Michael Rosen; "Dear Oscar" was first published in *Listening to a Pogrom on the Radio* (Smokestack Books, 2017) and also appeared in a slightly different